Everything You Need to Know About Credit

Why You Need it

How to get it

How to Use it

How to fix it

Why You Need it

There are five main reasons you need to establish and maintain good credit. Some of these reasons are obvious others not so much. Your ability to obtain and manage credit affects several aspects of your life. The most obvious is how you are treated when you want or need a loan. But credit affects much more than just your ability to get a loan and how much interest you will be charged. So, sit back and put on your learning cap. In this chapter we will explain each of the five reasons in detail.

Getting a Loan

When you want to get a loan (we'll cover financially sound reasons to borrow money in the third chapter) the lender will want evidence of your ability to repay that loan. They look at things like work history, how much money you earn, how much money you spend, and how much money you save. But they also look at how much money you have borrowed and paid back on time in the past.

Now this can create a dilemma for people who have not yet established a credit history. You need credit history to get credit to build credit history. I'll show you several ways to overcome that dilemma in the next chapter.

Getting Better Terms for your Loan

Having a good credit score is one of the most important factors in getting any type of financial assistance, there are institutions that are still willing to loan money to people with no credit, poor credit, and even bad credit. The problems you run into if you are in one of these categories are many. First, you will be required to provide more documentation for your loan. Secondly, you will also pay a much higher interest rate. This is how lenders balance the risks and rewards i.e. potential losses versus potential profits lending to you present.

The extra documentation is to reassure them that you have the means to repay the loan. They may require capital held in reserve, a co-signer, or other means of securing the loan. Consider the difference between a pawn shop, a payday lender, and a bank.

Pawn shops are used for short term loans by people who generally cannot get a loan anywhere else. The terms at pawn shops are heavily in favor of the shop. First you must give them something of value to hold as collateral against the loan. Second, they only loan you 20- 40 percent of the resale value of that item. So, let's say you need a hundred dollars for a few days. You would need to give them something worth two or three hundred dollars. Then when you repay the loan you will pay back principle plus interest. Pawn shop interest rates are among the highest around sometimes reaching as much as 23% per month. Let's say it takes you four months to pay back your hundred-dollar loan. Well, you would need $192 in this case to get your collateral back.

Another downside to Pawn shop loans is that even if you payback on time, you've done nothing to improve your credit rating for the next time you need a loan. A payday lender isn't much better either.

Payday lenders also charge ridiculous interest rates and fees for the loans they give. Although they have come under pressure lately to improve their practices, it is not uncommon for a person to pay on a loan for months or even years and still owe more than they originally borrowed.

If you want better interest rates to save yourself money, it is important to build good credit and keep your credit score high. I'll show you how to repair your credit score if it's broken in the last chapter. In the meantime, lets look at some more ways your credit can impact your life.

Getting and Keeping a Good Job

If you are working in an entry level position your employer is not likely to spend the resources necessary to check your credit report. However, if you are applying for a position with increased areas of responsibility they most likely will. To an employer having good credit is an indication of your reliability and sound decision-making skills. Good credit reflects good character. Employers may not necessarily see good credit as a positive, but they will see bad credit as a negative. This is especially true for jobs where the employer is trusting you with sensitive information or access to high value items. In the military, if you don't have good credit you cannot get a security clearance. And if you have a security clearance and develop bad credit, you will be at risk of losing not only the clearance but your job as well.

Automobile and Home Insurance

It is no secret that insurance companies use your credit score as a part of their actuary tables. They see greater risk insuring people with poor credit scores than with people with high credit scores. It's not that they are picking on you, but rather that experience has shown them that there is a correlation between their risk and your ability to gain and maintain good credit.

Your credit score can make a very big difference in your automobile and home insurance premiums. The difference in your premium can be significant. According to a [Consumer Reports study](), their single drivers who had "good" scores paid $68 to $526 more per year, on average, than similar drivers with the best scores. This varies by which State you live in, so I recommend you check out their report here and see what the impact would be on you.

The rates shown are the average new-customer premium for adult single drivers with a clean driving record and poor, good, or excellent credit. Compare these to the average premium for a driver with excellent credit and a driving while intoxicated!

Excellent	Good	Poor	Excellent w/ DWI
$965	$1198	$2266	$1367

In other words, you can have get convicted of driving while intoxicated and the insurance company still considers you a lower risk than someone with poor credit.

When it comes to home owner's insurance, if you have poor credit, you will pay up to three times more for the same insurance on the same house than a person with excellent credit. In a study done by Insurancequotes.com it was found that poor credit scores result in a significant increase in home owner insurance premiums as well. This is too substantial to ignore. If you have poor credit in Kansas, on average you will pay $3,900 more than a person with excellent credit for automobile and home insurance. That's about $325 per month in extra premiums. Let that sink in..

State	Average Premium	Percent Increase	Total
Kansas	$1431	182.16%	$4037.71

How to Get Credit

There are many ways to get credit if you are just starting out. As I am sure you can imagine, some ways are much better than others. In this chapter we will look at five ways to build credit. I will explain the pros and cons of each. Everyone's situation is different so only you can decide which way is best for you. It may be a combination of the three ways or it may be that one method appeals more to your lifestyle and needs. Let's dig in.

There are five basic ways to build credit. I will discuss each of these from the least favorable (for most people) to the most favorable (for most people). Because everyone's situation is different I cannot make a specific recommendation for you. However, if you will read about each of the methods you will be able to determine which one fits your situation best. At the end of the chapter I will explain how to obtain each. Once you have decided which on is best for you, you will have directions to follow for how to obtain that type of loan.

Apply for a secured credit card.

The nice thing about secured credit cards is that they allow you the convenience of building credit in a way that may not cost you any interest at all. If you are responsible with your money and don't buy things you cannot afford, this option may be the best for you. There are a few downsides to this method. First, if you charge more than you can pay off each month the interest rate will be much higher than for other options. Secondly if you are not disciplined in your spending habits, these cards can be the fastest way to financial trouble of any of our options. Thirdly, you will need capital to set aside as security.

Apply for a secured installment loan.

A secured installment loan will work similarly to

a secured credit card. It will require capital set aside as security for the loan. One of the benefits to this type of loan has over a secured credit card is that it can be used to purchase larger ticket items. Another benefit is that you won't have as high of an interest rate and your payments will be the same each month. A third benefit is that it is much easy introduction to responsible spending. Each month you pay will not only be building good credit, but it will also build good habits of responsibility. Money, you already have at the financial institution or can deposit, is used as the collateral for the loan. That money is locked from your use until you have repaid the loan,

Get a co-signer. Using a co-signer allows you to leverage another person's good credit to help you build yours. That is a huge advantage if you have a friend or relative who is willing to accept the risk of backing your loan. The co-signer agrees to be responsible to pay back the loan if you cannot pay. You won't need considerable collateral, you will enjoy a much lower interest rate and you will benefit from better terms than you otherwise would. This might be a good option for you if you need a loan for your first car or you are trying to rent an apartment or house before you've established any credit. don't meet the minimum income requirements for a loan; are self-employed; or have changed jobs recently.

The downside to using a co-signer is that you are putting friendships and family relations at risk. What happens if you can't pay your debt or rent? The bank will go after your co-signer. So, you could potentially damage not only your own credit, but your co-signer's as well. If you have a strong sense of personal responsibility and a willing co-signer, this could be a very good option for you.

Get credit for the rent you pay.

If you are renting a house or an apartment, paying your rent on time is a great way to build your credit. First, you need a place to live anyway so it's not an additional expense. Secondly, there are no interest charges. The downside to this is that not all landlords report your payments to the three credit agencies. Something to consider when looking for a place to rent is whether or not they will report your payments to help you build credit. I know of two companies that allow landlords to offer this service to their tenants. Rent Track is one and Rental Karma is the other. Rent Track is a service for landlords. As far as I know they don't have a search feature yet where you could find rentals near you that offer their service so you will just have to ask. Rental Karma, on the other hand allows you to report up to 24 months of past rental history yourself. There is a one-time verification fee of $25 and then it's only $6.95 per month for ongoing reporting and $5 per month for past reporting.

Apply for a credit builder savings and loan account.

I saved this method for last because I think in many cases, especially for the teenager just starting out, this is the best method of building credit. The way this works is that you pay the loan payments first and then you get the money at the end of the term. It works just like depositing money into a savings account, except that it will show up at the credit agencies like a loan. Here's how it works. You open an account. Select the payment you can afford each month. They range from $25 to $194 per month for 12 to 24 months. The lender opens a certificate of deposit with a bank. At the end of your loan, the proceeds of that certificate of deposit, along with the interest that it earned, are given to you. The only downside I see to this method is for people who need to borrow money now. The good news is that if you are trying to establish credit, so you can get a better loan in the future, this is a great way to get started.

How to Obtain a secured credit card

There are several ways to obtain a secured credit card. In my opinion though, the best way is to go to your local bank. Banking locally isn't all that it used to be, however, it still affords you the opportunity to build a relationship with a loan department. This can come in very handy when applying for future loans. If you already have a bank account with a local bank, call the loan department and make an appointment to speak with a loan officer. Explain that you are wanting to open a secured credit card account with the aim of building your credit. The loan officer will be able to assist you in setting up the required accounts and explaining the terms to you. You will have a better experience if you find a small local bank or credit union rather than one of the national banks

How to Obtain a secured installment loan

If you think a secured installment loan is the best option for you, I recommend you follow the same steps as described in getting a secured credit card. In my opinion, the best way is to go to your local bank. Call the bank's loan department and make an appointment to speak with a loan officer. Explain that you are wanting to apply for a credit building loan with the aim of building your credit. The loan officer will be able to assist you in setting up the required accounts and explaining the terms to you. As with the secured credit card, you will have a better experience if you find a small local bank or credit union rather than one of the national banks.

How to Obtain a loan with a co-signer

If using a co-signer is the option that makes best sense for you the first step is to find someone with good credit who is willing to help you out. Once you have a willing accomplice, have them help you shop for the loan and apply for it. As I mentioned earlier, this is a good option for someone who needs a loan for a specific purpose, such as buying their first car, or renting their first apartment.

How to obtain a credit builder savings and loan account

A credit builder savings and loan account can be obtained at a local bank or credit union as well. Another option is an online service called [self lender](). Self lender will deposit your loan into a certificate of deposit (CD). These generally earn a higher interest rate than a bank or credit union savings account. Once the balance is paid off, you get the proceeds of the CD. Visit selflender.com to learn more. While I do generally recommend using a local bank or credit union, Self Lender offers a couple of advantages you may want to consider. First they provide you with free access to your credit scores so you can monitor as they improve. Secondly, they provide free credit monitoring. Finally, they report to all three credit rating agencies each month. You can see your score improving after you've made only a few payments.

How to Use Credit Once You Have It

There are as many uses for credit as there are stars in the sky, however, there are only a few uses that are beneficial to your financial wellbeing. Here are some good reasons to use credit:

1) Establish Credit. You can't build a good credit history if you've never borrowed money.
2) Buy a car. If you can get by without one you will be much better off. However, an automobile is necessary for most people to get to work.
3) Buy a house. Home ownership isn't right for everyone. There are the pros and cons of owning a home versus renting. However, once you have determined that home ownership is for you, this is a purchase that taking a loan is appropriate (and most likely necessary).
4) Self-improvement. Investing in yourself is a smart use of time and money. Borrowing money to learn a new skill that will increase your income can be a smart way to leverage your good credit into an even better lifestyle.

How to Keep and Improve Your Good Credit Rating

There may be other instances when it's a good idea for you to borrow money, but these four are practically universal.

Now that you have good credit, it is important to keep it that way. Here are some guidelines for maintaining your reputation as a good risk to lenders:

1) Pay your bills on time – not just your loan and credit card payments, but your rent, insurance, medical bills, telephone, power, and water bills too. Bottom line, if you owe money pay it on time every time.
2) Don't borrow too much – lenders look at your loan to income ratio to determine if you are over-extended. The higher the ratio, the higher your

interest rates will be on any new loans. Get above 43% and you may not qualify for any loans at all. To determine your ratio, divide your monthly net income (income after taxes and withholdings) by your monthly debt payments.

3) Keep your credit use low – similar to the debt ratio, lenders will look at the percentage of available credit that you are carrying. For example, if you have a credit limit of $1,000 on a credit card and you carry a balance (never a good idea) of $200, your ratio is 20%. Anything above that will start negatively affecting your credit score.

4) Don't open up too many lines of credit – every time you apply for a loan, whether you accept it or not, the lender will check your credit report. One or two checks a year won't affect your score too badly, however, if you get several hits your score will go down. This makes it

difficult to shop for a loan because no lender will give you a quote without first pulling a credit check. This is onetime it is very advantageous to know your score. For example, you can ask the lender, "if my score is ___ what will the interest rate on this loan be?" You can also ask the lender if they will be making a "hard pull" on your credit. If they say yes, you may want to be sure you really want the loan before you agree to let them.

5) Once you open your first account, keep it as long as it makes sense. The reason is that the age of your credit is another factor that impacts your credit score. In other words, the longer you have demonstrated good financial responsibility, the better your credit rating.

6) Monitor your credit – all three agencies allow you to check your credit report once a year with no charge. You need to make it habit of doing this

every year to make sure that everything on your report is accurate. In the next chapter I will show you how to do that and how to dispute any inaccuracies.

How to Fix it

Credit Repair: How to Help Yourself

You see the advertisements in newspapers, on TV, and on the Internet. You hear them on the radio. You get fliers in the mail, and maybe even calls offering credit repair services. They all make the same claims:

"Credit problems? No problem!"

"We can remove bankruptcies, judgments, liens, and bad loans from your credit file forever!"

"We can erase your bad credit — 100% guaranteed."

"Create a new credit identity — legally."

The Federal Trade Commission (FTC) says do yourself a favor and save some money, too. Don't believe these claims: they're very likely signs of a scam. Indeed, attorneys at the nation's consumer protection agency say they've never seen a legitimate credit repair operation making those claims. The fact is there's no quick fix for creditworthiness. You can improve your credit report legitimately, but it takes time, a conscious effort, and sticking to a personal debt repayment plan.

Recognizing a Credit Repair Scam

Everyday, companies target consumers who have poor credit histories with promises to clean up their credit report, so they can get a car loan, a home mortgage, insurance, or even a job once they pay them a fee for the service. The truth is, these companies can't deliver an improved credit report for you using the tactics they promote. It's illegal: No one can remove accurate negative information from your credit report. So, after you pay them hundreds or thousands of dollars in fees, you're left with the same credit report and someone else has your money.

If you see a credit repair offer, here's how to tell if the company behind it is up to no good:

- The company wants you to pay for credit repair services before they provide any services. Under the Credit Repair Organizations Act, credit repair companies cannot require you to pay until they have completed the services they have promised.
- The company doesn't tell you your rights and what you can do for yourself for free.
- The company recommends that you do not contact any of the three major national credit reporting companies directly.
- The company tells you they can get rid of most or all the negative credit information in your credit report, even if that

information is accurate and current.
- The company suggests that you try to invent a "new" credit identity — and then, a new credit report — by applying for an Employer Identification Number to use instead of your Social Security number.
- The company advises you to dispute all the information in your credit report, regardless of its accuracy or timeliness.

If you follow illegal advice and commit fraud, you may find yourself in legal hot water, too: It's a federal crime to lie on a loan or credit application, to misrepresent your Social Security number, and to obtain an Employer Identification Number from the Internal Revenue Service under false pretenses. You could be charged and prosecuted for mail or wire fraud if you use the mail, telephone, or Internet to apply for credit and provide false information.

Your Rights Regarding Credit Repair

No one can legally remove accurate and timely negative information from a credit report. The law allows you to ask for an investigation of information in your file that you dispute as inaccurate or incomplete. There is no charge for this. Some people hire a company to investigate on their behalf, but anything a credit repair clinic can do legally, you can do for yourself at little or no cost. According to the Fair Credit Reporting Act (FCRA):

- You're entitled to a free report if a company takes "adverse action" against you, like denying your application for credit, insurance, or employment. You must ask for your report within 60 days of receiving notice of the action. The notice will give you the name, address, and phone number of the consumer reporting company. You're also entitled to one free report a year if you're unemployed and plan to look for a job within 60 days; if you're on welfare; or if your report is inaccurate because of fraud, including identity theft.

- Each of the nationwide consumer reporting companies — Equifax, Experian, and TransUnion — is required to provide you with a free copy of your credit report once every 12 months, if you ask for it. The three companies have a central website, a toll-free telephone number, and a mailing address for consumers to order the free annual credit reports the government entitles them to. To order, click on annualcreditreport.com, call 1-877-322-8228, or complete the Annual Credit Report Request Form and mail it to:

Annual Credit Report Request Service

P.O. Box 105281
Atlanta, GA 30348-5281

You can use the form in this brochure, or you can print it from ftc.gov/credit. You may order reports from each of the three consumer reporting companies at the same time, or you can stagger your requests, ordering one from each company throughout the year from the central address. Don't contact the three nationwide consumer reporting companies individually or at another address because you may end up paying for a report that you're entitled to get for free. In fact, each consumer reporting company may charge you up to $10.50 to purchase an additional copy of your report within a 12-month period.

- It doesn't cost anything to dispute mistakes or outdated items on your credit report. Under the FCRA, both the consumer reporting company and the information provider (that is, the person, company, or organization that provides information about you to a consumer reporting company) are responsible for correcting inaccurate or incomplete information in your report. To take advantage of all your rights under the FCRA, contact the consumer reporting company and the information provider.

Helping Yourself

Step 1: Tell the consumer reporting company, in writing, what information you think is inaccurate. Include copies (NOT originals) of any documents that support your position. In addition to providing your complete name and address, your letter should identify each item in your report you dispute; state the facts and the reasons you dispute the information and ask that it be removed or corrected. You may want to enclose a copy of your report and circle the items in question. Send your letter by certified mail, "return receipt requested," so you can document that the consumer reporting company received it. Keep copies of your dispute letter and enclosures. Your letter may look something like the one below.

Sample Dispute Letter

Date
Your Name
Your Address,
City, State, Zip Code

Complaint Department
Name of Company
Address
City, State, Zip Code

Dear Sir or Madam:

I am writing to dispute the following information in my file. The items I dispute also are encircled on the attached copy of the report I received.

This item (identify item(s) disputed by name of source, such as creditors or tax court, and identify type of item, such as credit account, judgment, etc.) is (inaccurate or incomplete) because (describe what is inaccurate or incomplete and why). I am requesting that the item be deleted (or request another specific change) to correct the information.

Enclosed are copies of (use this sentence if applicable and describe any enclosed documentation, such as payment records, court documents) supporting my position. Please investigate this (these) matter(s) and (delete or correct) the disputed item(s) as soon as possible.

Sincerely,
Your name

Enclosures: (List what you are enclosing.)

Consumer reporting companies must investigate the items you question within 30 days — unless they consider your dispute frivolous. They also must forward all the relevant data you provide about the inaccuracy to the organization that provided the information. After the information provider receives notice of a dispute from the consumer reporting company, it is required to investigate, review the relevant information, and report the results back to the consumer reporting company. If this investigation reveals that the disputed information is inaccurate, the information provider has to notify the nationwide consumer reporting companies, so they can correct it in your file.

When the investigation is complete, the consumer reporting company must give you the results in writing, too, and a free copy of your report if the dispute results in a change. If an item is changed or deleted, the consumer reporting company is not permitted to put the disputed information back in your file unless the information provider verifies that it is accurate and complete. The consumer reporting company also must send you written notice that includes the name, address, and phone number of the information provider. If you ask, the consumer reporting company must send notices of any correction to anyone who received your report in the past six months. You also can ask that a corrected copy of your report be sent to anyone who received a copy during the past two years for employment purposes.

If an investigation doesn't resolve your dispute with the consumer reporting company, you can ask that a statement of the dispute be included in your file and in future reports. You also can ask the consumer reporting company to provide your statement to anyone who received a copy of your report in the recent past. You can expect to pay for this service.

Step 2: Tell the creditor or other information provider, in writing, that you dispute an item. Be sure to include copies (NOT originals) of documents that support your position. Many providers specify an address for disputes. If the provider reports the item to a consumer reporting company, it must include a notice of your dispute. And if you are correct — that is, if the information is found to be inaccurate — the information provider may not report it again.

Reporting Accurate Negative Information

When negative information in your report is accurate, only the passage of time can assure its removal. A consumer reporting company can report most accurate negative information for seven years and bankruptcy information for 10 years. Information about an unpaid judgment against you can be reported for seven years or until the statute of limitations runs out, whichever is longer. To calculate the seven-year reporting period, start from the date the event took place. There is no time limit on reporting information about criminal convictions; information reported in response to your application for a job that pays more than $75,000 a year; and information reported because you've applied for more than $150,000 worth of credit or life insurance.

The Credit Repair Organizations Act

Credit repair organizations must give you a copy of the "Consumer Credit File Rights Under State and Federal Law" before you sign a contract. They also must give you a written contract that spells out your rights and obligations. Read these documents before you sign anything. And before signing, know that a credit repair company cannot:

- make false claims about their services
- charge you until they have completed the promised services
- perform any services until they have your signature on a written contract and have

completed a three-day waiting period. During this time, you can cancel the contract without paying any fees.

Before you sign a contract, be sure it specifies:

- the payment terms for services, including the total cost
- a detailed description of the services the company will perform
- how long it will take to achieve the result
- any guarantees the company offer
- the company's name and business address

Have You Been Victimized?

Many states have laws regulating credit repair companies. State law enforcement officials may be helpful if you've lost money to credit repair scams. Don't be embarrassed to report a problem with a credit repair company. While you may fear that contacting the government could make your problems worse, remember that laws are in place to protect you. Contact your local consumer affairs office or your state Attorney General (AGs). Many AGs have toll-free consumer hotlines; check the Blue Pages of your telephone directory for the phone number or www.naag.org for a list of state attorneys general.

If You Need Help

Just because you have a poor credit report doesn't mean you can't get credit. Creditors set their own standards, and not all look at your credit history the same way. Some may look only at recent years to evaluate you for credit, and they may give you credit if your bill-paying history has improved. It may be worthwhile to contact creditors informally to discuss their credit standards.

If you're not disciplined enough to create a workable budget and stick to it, to work out a repayment plan with your creditors, or to keep track of your mounting bills, you might consider contacting a credit counseling organization. Many credit counseling organizations are nonprofit and work with you to solve your financial problems. But remember that "nonprofit" status doesn't guarantee free, affordable, or even legitimate services. In fact, some credit counseling organizations — even some that claim non-profit status — may charge high fees or hide their fees by pressuring consumers to make "voluntary" contributions that only cause more debt.

Most credit counselors offer services through local offices, the Internet, or on the telephone. If possible, find an organization that offers in-person counseling. Many universities, military bases, credit unions, housing authorities, and branches of the U.S. Cooperative Extension Service operate nonprofit credit counseling programs. Your financial institution, local consumer protection agency, and friends and family also may be good sources of information and referrals.

If you are considering filing for bankruptcy, be aware that bankruptcy laws require that you get credit counseling from a government-approved organization within six months before you file for bankruptcy relief. You can find a state-by-state list of government-approved organizations at www.usdoj.gov/ust, the website of the U.S. Trustee Program. That's the organization within the U.S. Department of Justice that supervises bankruptcy cases and trustees. Be wary of credit counseling organizations that say they are government-approved, but do not appear on the list of approved organizations.

Reputable credit counseling organizations can advise you on managing your money and debts, help you develop a budget, and offer free educational materials and workshops. Their counselors are certified and trained in the areas of consumer credit, money and debt management, and budgeting. Counselors discuss your entire financial situation with you and can help you develop a personalized plan to solve your money problems. An initial counseling session typically lasts an hour, with an offer of follow-up sessions.

Do-It-Yourself Check-Up

Regardless of your credit history, financial advisors and consumer advocates recommend reviewing your credit report periodically for three important reasons:

1. The information in your credit report affects whether you can get a loan or insurance — and how much you will have to pay for it.
2. It's important to make sure the information is accurate, complete, and up-to-date before you apply for a loan for a major purchase like a house or car,

buy insurance, or apply for a job.
3. It can help you deter, detect and defend against identity theft. That's when someone uses your personal information — like your name, your Social Security number, or your credit card number — to commit fraud. Identity thieves may use your information to open a new credit card account in your name. Then, when they don't pay the bills, the delinquent account is reported on your credit report. Inaccurate information like that could affect your ability to get credit, insurance, or even a job.

For More Information

To learn how to improve your credit worthiness and find legitimate resources for low or no-cost help, please see the following publications at ftc.gov/credit.

- [Your Access to Free Credit Reports](#) — Explains why it is important to monitor your credit history, how to request a report, and how to dispute errors.
- [How to Dispute Credit Report Errors](#) — Explains how to dispute and correct inaccurate information in your credit report. Includes a sample dispute letter.
- [Building a Better Credit Report](#) — Learn how to legally improve your credit report, how to deal with debt, how to spot credit-related scams, and more.
- [Knee Deep in Debt](#) — Discusses options to help you get back in the black, including: realistic budgeting, credit counseling from a reputable organization, debt consolidation, or bankruptcy.
- [Fiscal Fitness: Choosing a Credit Counselor](#) — Defines debt repayment plans, explains the differences between secured and unsecured debt, and offers

questions to ask credit counseling agencies if you consider using their services.

The FTC works for the consumer to prevent fraudulent, deceptive, and unfair business practices in the marketplace and to provide information to help consumers spot, stop, and avoid them. To file a [complaint](#) or to get [free information on consumer issues](#), visit [ftc.gov](#) or call toll-free, 1-877-FTC-HELP (1-877-382-4357); TTY: 1-866-653-4261. The FTC enters consumer complaints into the [Consumer Sentinel Network](#), a secure online database and investigative tool used by hundreds of civil and criminal law enforcement agencies in the U.S. and abroad.

www.ingramcontent.com/pod-product-compliance
Lightning Source LLC
Chambersburg PA
CBHW030515220526
45464CB00006B/2811